THE POETRY OF NICKEL

The Poetry of Nickel

Walter the Educator™

SKB

Silent King Books a WhichHead Imprint

Copyright © 2023 by Walter the Educator™

All rights reserved. No part of this book may be reproduced in any manner whatsoever without written permission except in the case of brief quotations embodied in critical articles and reviews.

First Printing, 2023

Disclaimer
This book is a literary work; poems are not about specific persons, locations, situations, and/or circumstances unless mentioned in a historical context. This book is for entertainment and informational purposes only. The author and publisher offer this information without warranties expressed or implied. No matter the grounds, neither the author nor the publisher will be accountable for any losses, injuries, or other damages caused by the reader's use of this book. The use of this book acknowledges an understanding and acceptance of this disclaimer.

"Earning a degree in chemistry changed my life!"
– Walter the Educator

dedicated to all the chemistry lovers, like myself, across the world

CONTENTS

Dedication v

Why I Created This Book? 1

One - Nickel, The Element 2

Two - Eternal Embrace 4

Three - Touches And Renews 6

Four - Metal Rare 8

Five - Symbol Of Fame 10

Six - Catalyst Divine 12

Seven - Nickel, Oh Nickel 14

Eight - Unwavering And Strong 16

Nine - Protective Charm 18

Ten - Wealth And Pride 20

Eleven - Element So Fine 22

Twelve - Endurance And Love 24

Thirteen - Play Many Roles	. . . . .	26
Fourteen - Power So Great	. . . . .	28
Fifteen - Do Conform	. . . . .	30
Sixteen - Malleable And Divine	. . . . .	32
Seventeen - Brilliantly Fine	. . . . .	34
Eighteen - Conduct With Ease	. . . . .	36
Nineteen - Marvel That Pervades	. . . . .	38
Twenty - Metal Of Significance	. . . . .	40
Twenty-One - Reign Supreme	. . . . .	42
Twenty-Two - Hold In Our Hand	. . . . .	44
Twenty-Three - Gleaming Grace	. . . . .	46
Twenty-Four - Lustrous Sheen	. . . . .	48
Twenty-Five - Big And Small	. . . . .	50
Twenty-Six - Conductor Of Electricity	. . . .	52
Twenty-Seven - Plating And Coatings	. . . . .	54
Twenty-Eight - Full Of Grace	. . . . .	56
Twenty-Nine - Marvel Of Chemistry	. . . .	58
Thirty - Majestic Gown	. . . . .	60
Thirty-One - Technology And Industry	. . . .	62
Thirty-Two - Steadfast And Pure	. . . . .	64

Thirty-Three - Beauty So Fine	. . . .	66
Thirty-Four - Mysteries Unfold	. . . .	68
Thirty-Five - Aerospace And Medicine	. . .	70
Thirty-Six - Hidden Gem	. . . .	72
About The Author	. . . .	74

WHY I CREATED THIS BOOK?

Creating a poetry book about the chemical element of Nickel was an interesting and unique approach to exploring the world of science through art. Nickel, with its distinct properties and significance in various industries, provides a rich source of inspiration for poetic expression. By delving into the characteristics, history, and applications of Nickel, I can weave together themes of strength, durability, versatility, and transformation. This fusion of science and poetry can captivate readers, sparking their curiosity about the natural world and fostering a deeper appreciation for the beauty and complexity of the periodic table.

ONE

NICKEL, THE ELEMENT

In the realm of metals, where power resides,
There dwells a character, born of fiery tides.
Nickel, they call it, a lustrous embrace,
With secrets and stories, it holds in its space.

A guardian of strength, steadfast and true,
Nickel, the element, shines in its hue.
A warrior of alloys, it blends and imparts,
Resilience and toughness to all of its parts.

From coins in our pockets to steel so grand,
Nickel's touch adorns creations by hand.
Its presence, unyielding, in every frame,
Endowing strength to withstand the flame.

In the depths of the Earth, where it lay,
Nickel, the wanderer, found its own way.

From sulfide ores, it emerged with grace,
Revealing its beauty, in each trace.
 A catalyst, it dances with chemistry's might,
Aiding reactions, as day turns to night.
Electroplating, it weaves a fine spell,
Bestowing charm on objects so well.
 Oh, Nickel, the enigma, with secrets untold,
A silent observer, with tales yet unfold.
Its magnetic allure, a force to behold,
Captivating hearts, both young and old.
 In every corner, in every stride,
Nickel, the element, walks by our side.
With strength and resilience, it lights up the way,
Guiding us through, with each passing day.

TWO

ETERNAL EMBRACE

In the heart of the Earth, where secrets lie,
There dwells a silent strength, a metal known as Nickel.
A warrior in disguise, with a spirit so high,
It shines in the darkness, a gleaming miracle.

Nickel, a force of resilience, unyielding and tough,
Forged in the depths of our planet's core.
From ancient times to modern stuff,
Its presence felt, from shore to shore.

Oh, Nickel, you bring value to our minted coins,
A symbol of wealth, a treasure to behold.
Your metallic embrace, a mark that joins,
The hands of commerce, as stories are told.

But beyond the currency, your power extends,
To the realm of steel, where strength is born.

With heat and pressure, the metal transcends,
Forging structures robust, that shall not be torn.

    And in the realm of chemistry, you play your part,
An element of intrigue, a catalyst of change.
A catalyst, so versatile, that sparks a start,
In reactions that dance, your influence remains.

    Oh, Nickel, you enchant us with your magnetism,
Drawing us closer, with an irresistible force.
Your mysteries unfold, a cosmic prism,
Guiding us through life's journey, staying on course.

    Nickel, a guardian, a companion true,
A metal that endures, through time and space.
In every atom, a piece of you,
A testament to your might, an eternal embrace.

THREE

TOUCHES AND RENEWS

In the realm of steel, its brilliance gleams,
A metal of might, Nickel, it seems.
With strength and resilience, it stands tall,
In every corner, it touches us all.

From coins in our pockets, jingling with glee,
To bridges and buildings, strong as can be.
Nickel, the currency of value and worth,
Guiding our journey on this vast Earth.

A catalyst it becomes in chemistry's dance,
Unleashing reactions, giving them a chance.
From hydrogenation to catalytic cracking,
Nickel's versatility, there's no lacking.

In alloys and plating, it finds its place,
Enhancing the beauty, adding a grace.

With a touch of Nickel, objects come alive,
A shimmering touch, where wonders thrive.
    From batteries to magnets, it powers our needs,
A magnetic allure, as it subtly leads.
Nickel, the element, a treasure untold,
A story of wonder, waiting to unfold.
    Oh, Nickel, you shine with a radiant glow,
A symbol of strength, wherever you go.
From deep in the Earth to the heavens above,
You guide us with grace, with your endless love.
    So let us embrace this metal so true,
In every aspect, it touches and renews.
Nickel, the element that lights up our path,
A companion, a friend, in the aftermath.

FOUR

METAL RARE

In the realm of metals, bold and bright,
An element commands our sight,
With strength and resilience, it shines,
A treasure hidden in Earth's confines.

Nickel, the faithful ally we keep,
In our lives, its presence runs deep,
From coins that jingle in our hand,
To tools that shape and shape the land.

In steel's embrace, it finds a home,
Forged in fires, it stands alone,
A catalyst for strength and might,
In structures that pierce the sky's height.

Chemistry's dance, it does partake,
In compounds, reactions it does wake,

A catalyst, a catalyst true,
In laboratories, it breaks through.
    Magnetic allure, it holds within,
Drawing us close, it does begin,
To explore the mysteries untold,
In fields where magnets do unfold.
    Oh, Nickel, you guide and inspire,
A metal that sets our hearts afire,
With versatility, you enchant,
Creating alloys, a master's chant.
    In plating, you bring a shining grace,
Adorning objects with your embrace,
And in batteries, you hold the power,
To light up the darkest hour.
    Nickel, you are a metal rare,
With boundless potential, oh so fair,
In your presence, we find delight,
A testament to nature's might.

FIVE

SYMBOL OF FAME

In the realm of coins, it does shine bright,
Nickel, a metal that catches the light,
Its silvery hue, a reflection of grace,
A symbol of value, in every embrace.

But beyond the realm of currency's might,
Nickel, a secret, hidden from sight,
A catalyst it plays, in chemistry's game,
Unleashing reactions, with a fiery flame.

Its atoms dance, in compounds they dwell,
In molecules intricate, where stories they tell,
From batteries to pigments, it plays its part,
A chemical wizard, with a creative heart.

Magnetic allure, it holds in its core,
Drawing the iron, with an invisible force,

In steel it resides, strengthening the frame,
A pillar of strength, a symbol of fame.
    Oh, Nickel, a metal of many a guise,
From coins to catalysts, it does arise,
A versatile element, with tales to unfold,
Forever entwined, in the stories of old.

SIX

CATALYST DIVINE

In the realm of elements, a gem does reside,
With strength and allure, it cannot hide,
Nickel, oh Nickel, a metal so grand,
A catalyst of change, in every land.

Its presence is subtle, yet mighty and true,
In reactions it sparks, creating the new,
From hydrogenation to cracking of oil,
Nickel's hand guides, with expertise and toil.

In commerce it thrives, a coin of great worth,
A symbol of value, a treasure from birth,
From pennies to dimes, its shimmering hue,
Nickel, oh Nickel, we honor you.

In steel's mighty forge, it plays a key role,
Strengthening the alloy, giving it soul,

A guardian of structures, steadfast and strong,
Nickel, oh Nickel, our protector from wrong.
    In chemistry's realm, it dances with grace,
A catalyst supreme, in every embrace,
Facilitating reactions, with magical touch,
Nickel, oh Nickel, we thank you so much.
    So versatile and magnetic, it holds a great charm,
In batteries and alloys, it causes no harm,
A conductor of energy, it powers the world,
Nickel, oh Nickel, our stalwart unfurled.
    With value unmatched, in a league of its own,
A catalyst divine, its worth clearly shown,
Nickel, oh Nickel, we sing you this praise,
Forever our guiding light, in all of our days.

SEVEN

NICKEL, OH NICKEL

In a realm of elements, shining bright,
There exists a metal, a captivating sight,
Nickel, oh Nickel, a beauty so rare,
With a lustrous charm, beyond compare.

Magnetic whispers dance upon its surface,
Drawing hearts closer, with a force so purpose,
Attracting the curious, the seekers of truth,
Nickel's magnetic pull, a testament to its youth.

A catalyst it becomes, in the realm of chemistry,
Sparkling reactions, transforming the ordinary,
Catalyzing change, with a touch so light,
Nickel, the alchemist, turning darkness to light.

Oh Nickel, you're a symbol of strength,
Endurance unmatched, spanning endless length,

Through trials and tribulations, you stand tall,
Guiding and inspiring, as you never falter or fall.

In the forge of creation, you play your part,
Forged in fire, a guardian of the heart,
Protecting against corrosion, a shield so strong,
Nickel, the guardian, singing its protective song.

Versatile and adaptable, you wear many hats,
From coins to alloys, you're where it all starts,
A warrior of elements, a pillar of pride,
Nickel, oh Nickel, forever by our side.

EIGHT

UNWAVERING AND STRONG

In the realm of elements, a silent might resides,
A metal so versatile, with strength that abides.
Nickel, the guardian of reactions untold,
A catalyst of change, a story yet unfold.

    Within its core, a magnetic force so grand,
Drawing in the currents with a steady hand.
From alloys it weaves, a tapestry of might,
Binding together worlds, forging futures bright.

    Its presence in coins, a symbol of wealth,
A guardian of value, protecting the self.
In jewelry it gleams, a shimmering embrace,
Adorning souls with grace, leaving hearts in chase.

    Nickel, the compass, guiding our way,
Through the tempest of life, in darkness and gray.

Its beauty, a beacon, a light in the night,
Leading us forward, with courage and might.
   Oh, Nickel, the catalyst of change and growth,
A guardian, a protector, a steadfast oath.
Enduring the ages, unwavering and strong,
In your presence, we find where we belong.

NINE

PROTECTIVE CHARM

In the realm of chemistry, a catalyst supreme,
There lies a metal, a mystical dream.
Nickel, the element, with powers untold,
A magnetism within, a tale to behold.
    A catalyst of change, it sparks the reaction,
Unveiling transformations, a chemical attraction.
In the crucible of science, it dances with delight,
Empowering reactions, in the depths of the night.
    A conductor of power, with electrons it weaves,
In batteries and alloys, its versatility cleaves.
From stainless steel's embrace to a guitar's sweet sound,
Nickel's presence in all, forever renowned.
    A guardian it becomes, a symbol of strength,
Resistant to corrosion, it goes to great lengths.

In coins and armor, it shields us from harm,
A guardian of value, a protective charm.
   But beyond its might, lies a secret unseen,
Nickel, the element, a catalyst serene.
A catalyst of change, in nature's grand design,
Guiding transformations, like a poet's line.
   So let us marvel at Nickel's allure,
A catalyst, a guardian, steadfast and pure.
In the realm of chemistry, its story unfurled,
Nickel, the element, changing the world.

TEN

WEALTH AND PRIDE

In the realm of chemistry, Nickel is hailed,
A catalyst, its powers truly unveiled.
With electrons dancing, magnetic in its sway,
A metal that captures the light of day.

Oh, Nickel, the element so versatile,
In batteries and alloys, you bring a smile.
Powering the world, in every cell and wire,
Your presence, Nickel, sets our hearts on fire.

With strength unmatched, you protect from corrosion,
A shield against decay, a guardian in every occasion.
In bridges and buildings, you stand tall and strong,
Nickel, the defender, we rely on you for long.

But beyond your might, a beauty lies within,
In coins and jewelry, your allure does begin.

A guiding force, a symbol of wealth and pride,
Nickel, you shine bright, never to hide.
    And in stainless steel, your presence is supreme,
A catalyst of change, a part of every dream.
Transforming the ordinary into something grand,
Nickel, the catalyst, forever you shall stand.
    Oh, Nickel, the element of wonder and might,
In every facet of life, you shine so bright.
From catalyst to protector, from beauty to strength,
Your presence, Nickel, resonates at length.

ELEVEN

ELEMENT SO FINE

In a world of elements, Nickel stands tall,
A versatile metal, admired by all.
With strength and shine, it holds its own,
A catalyst of change, its power is known.
    From coins to batteries, its uses abound,
In alloys and plating, it can be found.
A protective shield, it never fails,
Resisting corrosion, it prevails.
    With a magnetic charm, it draws the eye,
A symbol of strength, it can't deny.
In catalytic reactions, it plays a role,
Speeding up processes, with control.
    Nickel, oh Nickel, a metal so grand,
In chemistry's realm, you firmly stand.

Your presence is felt, in every domain,
A catalyst for progress, in its purest strain.
    From industry to art, you leave your mark,
In buildings and sculptures, so bright and stark.
A conductor of heat, a conductor of light,
Nickel, dear Nickel, you shine so bright.
    So let us celebrate, this element so fine,
For its properties and uses, truly divine.
Nickel, the metal, that can't be denied,
In the realm of elements, you'll forever abide.

TWELVE

ENDURANCE AND LOVE

In the depths of the Earth, where darkness prevails,
Lies a metal, strong and enduring, that never fails.
Oh, Nickel, a marvel of strength and might,
A guardian of secrets, hidden from sight.

With a heart of steel and a soul so pure,
You shield us from harm, of that I am sure.
In alloys and mixtures, you lend your grace,
A catalyst for progress, in every place.

From coins and cutlery to skyscrapers high,
Your presence is felt, as the days go by.
A symbol of value, a treasure untold,
Your worth is priceless, more than silver or gold.

Through fire and heat, you stand tall and true,
Unyielding and steadfast, like the ocean's blue.

In laboratories, you dance and ignite,
A symphony of reactions, a mesmerizing sight.
  Oh, Nickel, you are a master of transformation,
Shaping our world with your divine creation.
From the depths of the Earth to the stars above,
You are a testament to endurance and love.
  So let us raise a toast to Nickel's might,
A metal so noble, shining ever bright.
May your presence be felt in every corner and nook,
Forever a symbol of strength and rebirth, you took.

THIRTEEN

PLAY MANY ROLES

Nickel, oh Nickel, you shine so bright,
A metal that's useful in different ways, quite.
In alloys, coins, and jewelry, you play a part,
Adding strength and beauty, you're a work of art.

A catalyst for change, you speed up reactions,
Your presence in batteries and electroplating is no abstraction.
Transforming energy, you're a conductor of electricity,
Your electrons flowing freely, with such simplicity.

Oh Nickel, you symbolize worth and value,
Your endurance and resilience, never to subdue.
A key component in many machines and tools,
Your strength and durability, never to be fooled.

In meteorites, you're found in rare form,
A remnant of the universe, a cosmic norm.

In the Earth's core, you're a part of the mix,
Your magnetic properties, a geological fix.
   Nickel, oh Nickel, you're a versatile element,
With properties that make you so relevant.
From catalyst to conductor, you play many roles,
Enduring and transformative, you touch many souls.

FOURTEEN

POWER SO GREAT

In the depths of the earth, it lies,
A metal with a strength that belies,
Its beauty and its catalytic power,
Nickel, a treasure that we scour.

From coins to jewelry, it shines bright,
A metal that endures through the night,
Its value, more than just its worth,
A transformative force on this Earth.

Nickel, a conductor of electricity,
A versatile metal, of great utility,
Its endurance, a symbol of resilience,
A metal that defies all hindrance.

Oh, Nickel, a true wonder of nature,
A metal that we all should treasure,

For in it lies a power so great,
A power that we can never underestimate.

FIFTEEN

DO CONFORM

Nickel, oh Nickel, your presence so grand
A catalyst for reactions, so perfectly planned
In the refining of oil, you play a key role
Aiding in the process to reach a high goal
    From coins to alloys, you're used far and wide
In stainless steel products, you never subside
A protective layer, you provide with pride
Rust and corrosion, you do easily hide
    Your properties, oh Nickel, are truly unique
Malleable and ductile, you form without critique
A magnetic force, you proudly exude
Conductivity high, you never elude
    Oh Nickel, how valuable you truly are
Endurance and strength, you never do mar

Transforming with ease, you shine like a star
A chemical element, you're truly bizarre
   Nickel, oh Nickel, how versatile you are
From batteries to wires, you're never too far
A conductor of electricity, you truly excel
In so many domains, you truly do dwell
   Oh Nickel, how beautiful you truly are
Your strength and shine, they never do mar
Transforming with ease, you take on new form
A chemical element, you never do conform

SIXTEEN

MALLEABLE AND DIVINE

In the realm of elements, Nickel shines bright,
A metal so versatile, a celestial light.
With an atomic number of twenty-eight,
Its properties make it truly great.

Nickel, oh Nickel, a lustrous alloy,
A symbol of strength, a symbol of joy.
Resistant to corrosion, it stands strong,
Enduring the test of time, all along.

From stainless steel to batteries galore,
Nickel's uses, oh, they never bore.
In coins and in plating, it finds its place,
A metal of value, a metal with grace.

Oh, Nickel, the conductor supreme,
Electricity flows through you, like a dream.

With conductivity high, you conduct with ease,
Transmitting power, bringing life to these seas.
　From guitar strings to electrical wires,
Nickel's conductive nature never tires.
In magnets and alloys, it finds its role,
A metal so versatile, it touches the soul.
　Oh, Nickel, malleable and divine,
Your beauty, oh, it truly shines.
From jewelry to sculptures, you're shaped with grace,
A metal of art, a metal embraced.
　With your silvery hue and your radiant glow,
Nickel, you captivate, a sight to behold.
In the world of elements, you stand apart,
A metal of wonder, a masterpiece of art.

SEVENTEEN

BRILLIANTLY FINE

In the realm of elements, Nickel stands tall,
A conductor of energy, it does enthral.
With electrons dancing in its atomic core,
Its conductivity, a marvel to explore.
    Oh, Nickel, transformer of humble might,
Through alloys and plating, you shine so bright.
From coins in pockets to wires in flight,
Your transformative properties ignite.
    With strength and endurance, Nickel prevails,
In stainless steel, it never fails.
Resistant to corrosion, it weathers the test,
A versatile metal, it's truly the best.
    Oh, Nickel, precious and rare,
Your value, beyond compare.

Magnetic in nature, you draw us near,
A lustrous metal, forever held dear.
   Through your conductive power, electricity flows,
Bringing life to our devices, from highs to lows.
From batteries to circuits, you spark the flame,
Nickel, the conductor, forever in our name.
   So, let us celebrate this element divine,
Nickel, the conductor, so brilliantly fine.
In its conductivity, it lights up our days,
A metal that sparks wonder in myriad ways.

EIGHTEEN

CONDUCT WITH EASE

Nickel, oh Nickel, you shine so bright,
A conductor of electricity, a wondrous sight.
Your transformative properties we cannot ignore,
You bring life to objects, you're a conductor at the core.

Your conductivity is what makes you unique,
A metal so versatile, it's hard not to speak
Of your ability to transform and endure,
From coins to batteries, you're so pure.

Your magnetic properties are a sight to see,
An alloy with iron, how wonderful can that be.
From stainless steel to musical instruments,
Your versatility and endurance are evident.

Nickel, oh Nickel, your significance we cannot deny,
A metal so important, it's hard to pass by.

From plating to alloys, you play a vital role,
In our daily lives, you bring warmth to our soul.
   Your resistance to corrosion is what sets you apart,
An element so strong, it's hard to depart.
From wires to electrodes, you conduct with ease,
Nickel, oh Nickel, you bring life to everything you seize.

NINETEEN

MARVEL THAT PERVADES

In the realm of elements, there lies a star,
A metal that shines bright, both near and far.
With strength and beauty, it catches the eye,
Nickel, the element that never shall die.
    Versatile it is, in many a way,
A conductor of heat, it is known to stay.
Electrical currents, it eagerly conducts,
Through wires and circuits, its power erupts.
    Enduring and steadfast, in every test,
Nickel prevails, it outshines the rest.
Resistant to corrosion, a shield it wears,
Protecting from rust, it shows no wear and tears.
    From coins to pipes, to materials galore,
Nickel's presence is felt, from shore to shore.

In alloys it blends, its strength it imparts,
Creating structures, from bridges to arts.
    Oh Nickel, thy radiance never fades,
A gem among metals, a marvel that pervades.
In its vibrant essence, we find delight,
Forever it shines, in our world so bright.

TWENTY

METAL OF SIGNIFICANCE

In the realm of elements, there lies Nickel's grace,
A conductor of energy, with elegance and embrace.
With atomic number twenty-eight, it shines so bright,
A metal of versatility, a symbol of might.

Oh, Nickel, you possess conductivity's art,
Transferring electrons with a skillful spark.
From wires to circuits, you bring power's flow,
Guiding electricity wherever it may go.

With strength and resilience, you withstand the test,
Resisting corrosion, you're truly the best.
In coins and jewelry, your beauty does gleam,
A symbol of wealth, a metal of esteem.

In industries vast, you find your rightful place,
From aerospace to batteries, you leave your trace.

In stainless steel and alloys, you lend your might,
Enhancing strength and durability, shining so bright.

    Oh, Nickel, you're a magnet, pulling hearts near,
Attracting admiration, with a magnetic sphere.
Transforming properties, you possess in your core,
An element of wonder, forever to adore.

    So let us celebrate, this element divine,
Nickel, oh Nickel, forever you'll shine.
In science and industry, your presence we see,
A metal of significance, forever to be.

TWENTY-ONE

REIGN SUPREME

In the realm of elements, behold Nickel's might,
A metal that gleams with an ethereal light.
Its conductivity, a mesmerizing dance,
Weaving currents with an enchanting trance.

    Versatile and strong, it weathers the storm,
Enduring in alloys, a foundation to form.
From stainless steel's embrace to guitar's sweet sound,
Nickel's presence in art is truly renowned.

    A conductor of electricity, it conducts the flow,
Harnessing energy with an electric glow.
In circuits and wires, it hums with delight,
Guiding electrons through the darkest of night.

    Resistance to corrosion, a shield it maintains,
Defying the ravages of time's relentless rains.

Through rust and decay, it stands tall and true,
A guardian of purity, unyielding and blue.

In magnets it finds its magnetic allure,
Drawing metal to metal, with a force so pure.
Nickel's magnetic charm, a secret it keeps,
Binding and pulling, a connection that seeps.

In coins and in jewelry, it adorns with grace,
A symbol of wealth and elegance, in every place.
Science and industry, its domain so vast,
Nickel's significance, forever will last.

Oh, Nickel, you shimmer with beauty untold,
A metal of wonder, precious and bold.
In the realm of elements, you reign supreme,
Nickel, a treasure, in every gleam.

TWENTY-TWO

HOLD IN OUR HAND

In the realm of elements, there's one shining bright,
A metal that defies corrosion's might.
Nickel, oh Nickel, a treasure so rare,
With qualities unique, beyond compare.

A conductor of electricity, it takes the lead,
Through wires and circuits, its power does feed.
In industries vast, it finds its place,
From electronics to coins, it leaves its trace.

Oh, Nickel, you're versatile, in more ways than one,
In stainless steel, you lend strength, never undone.
With alloys and plating, your presence is felt,
In cars and airplanes, where durability is dealt.

Endurance is your virtue, unwavering and true,
Magnetic attraction, in all that you do.

From magnets to batteries, you play a part,
In technology's realm, you hold a special heart.
   Oh, Nickel, your beauty shines through and through,
A lustrous metal, with a gleam so true.
Resisting rust and decay, you stand tall,
In science and industry, you conquer all.
   So let us celebrate, this metal so grand,
Nickel, the element, that we hold in our hand.
From strength to conductivity, you lead the way,
Nickel, oh Nickel, forever here to stay.

TWENTY-THREE

GLEAMING GRACE

In the realm of metals, a shining star,
Lies a treasure called Nickel, both near and far.
With magnetic allure, it pulls with might,
Drawing hearts and minds like a celestial light.
    Resistant to corrosion, it stands tall,
A guardian against nature's call.
Through wind and rain, it remains unscathed,
A testament to its strength, forever engraved.
    In industries wide, its uses unfold,
From stainless steel to coins of gold.
A versatile companion, reliable and true,
In every endeavor, it shines anew.
    Endurance its virtue, a flame that won't fade,
Through trials and tribulations, it's never swayed.

Like a warrior in battle, it withstands the test,
A symbol of resilience, it stands among the best.

    Conductor of currents, a spark of life,
In every circuit, it banishes strife.
With electrons dancing, a symphony of power,
Nickel conducts with grace, hour after hour.

    Oh, Nickel, you dazzle with gleaming grace,
A metal of beauty, a lasting embrace.
In coins and jewelry, your presence reigns,
A testament to your worth, that forever remains.

    So let us celebrate, this elemental king,
With strength and endurance, it continues to bring.
In science and industry, its legacy so pure,
Nickel, the metal that will forever endure.

TWENTY-FOUR

LUSTROUS SHEEN

In the depths of Earth's embrace, Nickel lies,
A metal of strength, enduring and wise.
Its magnetic allure, a force untold,
Drawing souls closer, binding them bold.

In the forge of time, Nickel's essence gleams,
With steadfast resolve, it withstands extremes.
Through fire and ice, it stands tall and true,
A testament to resilience, ever anew.

In industries vast, Nickel finds its place,
From batteries to turbines, its embrace.
In science and tech, its importance is clear,
A catalyst for progress, year after year.

A shield against rust, corrosion's cruel bite,
Nickel's armor resists, shining so bright.
In alloys it mingles, creating a blend,
Strength and malleability, a perfect trend.

In plating, it adorns with a lustrous sheen,
A touch of elegance, a sight to be seen.
Its conductivity, a pathway of flow,
Electrons dance freely, a cosmic show.

And when challenges come, Nickel stands tall,
A symbol of resilience, it won't ever fall.
For in its core lies a beauty untold,
A metal of endurance, a story unfold.

Oh, Nickel, dear Nickel, forever we sing,
Of your lasting impact, your enduring spring.
In the tapestry of elements, you shine,
A testament to nature's grand design.

TWENTY-FIVE

BIG AND SMALL

In the realm of elements, a star shines bright,
A symbol of strength, endurance, and might,
Nickel, the metal, so precious and true,
With properties that make it stand out anew.

Oh, Nickel, your magnetic allure,
Draws us close, like a love so pure,
Attracting hearts with an irresistible force,
Binding us together, in a cosmic course.

From coins to alloys, you play a crucial role,
In industries and technologies, you set the goal,
Your beauty, so radiant, in every form you take,
A testament to science and the risks we undertake.

In catalysis, you lend a helping hand,
Unlocking reactions, as if by command,
Your presence, a catalyst, ignites the flame,
Transforming the ordinary, leaving us forever changed.

Oh, Nickel, your resilience is a sight to behold,
Against rust and decay, you stand bold,
A guardian of structures, steadfast and strong,
Defying the elements, proving them wrong.

Conductive and versatile, you pave the way,
In electrical circuits, where currents play,
Transmitting power, connecting us all,
A conduit of energy, both big and small.

Nickel, oh Nickel, you're a treasure untold,
In science, industry, and stories of old,
Forever you'll shine, in our history's page,
A symbol of progress, a symbol of age.

So let us raise a toast, to Nickel's might,
A metal so noble, a shining light,
For in its essence, we find a truth,
That strength and beauty lie in the pursuit.

TWENTY-SIX

CONDUCTOR OF ELECTRICITY

In the realm of elements, there lies a noble metal,
With a lustrous sheen, a radiance so ethereal.
Nickel, the name that echoes through time,
A precious gem, a treasure so sublime.

Its beauty, a dance of silver hues,
Reflecting light with a captivating muse.
Magnetic whispers in its atomic heart,
Drawing souls close, never to be torn apart.

In science and industry, it finds its worth,
A catalyst for progress, a catalyst for mirth.
Endurance is its virtue, resistance its creed,
Against rust and decay, it takes the lead.

In technology's embrace, it finds its home,
Powering the world, wherever we may roam.

With strength unmatched, it weathers the storm,
A beacon of hope, a shield so warm.

Conductor of electricity, its glory unfurled,
Connecting lives, a conductor of the world.
Challenges it bears with unwavering might,
In the face of adversity, it shines so bright.

Oh, Nickel, guardian of the flame,
Malleable and elegant, you rise to acclaim.
In plating, you adorn with grace and flair,
A shield against corrosion, a guardian so rare.

So let us raise a toast to this element divine,
Nickel, the star that will forever shine.
In beauty, resilience, and versatility untold,
Its enduring impact, a story to be told.

TWENTY-SEVEN

PLATING AND COATINGS

In the realm of metals, a gem gleams bright,
A lustrous element, Nickel's might.
Its magnetic allure, a captivating trait,
Drawing hearts together, sealing fate.

In industries vast, Nickel finds its place,
An alloy companion, a metal's embrace.
From stainless steel to coins in a hand,
Its presence is felt, a symbol grand.

Endurance its virtue, unwavering and true,
With strength unmatched, it sees us through.
In turbines it spins, in engines it roars,
A testament to resilience, forever it soars.

Technology's ally, a conductor supreme,
In wires and circuits, it reigns supreme.

From smartphones to cars, it powers our lives,
A marvel of science, where progress thrives.
    A guardian against rust, decay's vile kin,
Nickel's resistance, a battle it will win.
In plating and coatings, it safeguards with grace,
Preserving beauty, leaving no trace.
    Oh, Nickel, conductor of electricity's flow,
With every charge, your power does show.
A symbol of resilience, a metal divine,
In your presence, strength we find.
    So let us celebrate, this element so rare,
Nickel, the jewel, beyond compare.
In its shimmering essence, we find delight,
A testament to nature's alchemical might.

TWENTY-EIGHT

FULL OF GRACE

In alloys it shines, a metal so bold,
A touch of nickel, worth more than gold.
Mix it with iron, make steel so strong,
Withstanding the test, when things go wrong.

Plating the surfaces, a gleaming delight,
Nickel's allure, a shimmering sight.
Adorning the cars, the planes in the sky,
Its durability, it will never deny.

A catalyst for change, a silent force,
Nickel's presence, a magnetic source.
In technology's grasp, it plays its part,
Connecting the circuits, igniting the spark.

An element of endurance, it stands the test,
Against time's trials, it's always blessed.

With rust-resistant armor, it never corrodes,
In the face of decay, it forever erodes.
  Coins and jewelry, a touch of class,
Nickel's conductivity, unsurpassed.
A conductor of current, it lights the way,
Powering the world, day after day.
  So let us celebrate this metal so fine,
Nickel, the element that will forever shine.
With strength and resilience, it takes its place,
A versatile element, full of grace.

TWENTY-NINE

MARVEL OF CHEMISTRY

In the depths of earth, there lies a treasure,
A metal of strength, beyond measure.
Nickel, the element, so steadfast and true,
With qualities rare, that astound and imbue.

A guardian against rust and decay,
Nickel resists, come what may.
Like a fortress, it stands, unwavering and bold,
Protecting the secrets that it holds.

Conductor of electricity, with impeccable might,
Nickel conducts, with all its light.
Through wires and circuits, it weaves its way,
Powering the world, night and day.

In the realm of chemistry, it takes its place,
With elegance and grace, it leaves its trace.

Malleable and ductile, it bends to the will,
Crafted into wonders, it never stands still.
   Its shimmering surface, an ethereal sight,
Reflecting the sun's golden light.
A testament to its beauty and charm,
Nickel, the element, with a heart so warm.
   So let us celebrate this metal divine,
For its strength and endurance, we shall enshrine.
Connecting lives, powering technology,
Nickel, the element, a marvel of chemistry.

THIRTY

MAJESTIC GOWN

In the realm of chemistry, a marvel lies,
A metal rare, with beauty that defies,
Its name is Nickel, strong and bold,
A story untold, waiting to unfold.

A symbol of strength, it stands the test,
Against rust and decay, it's truly blessed,
A shield against time, it never corrodes,
Resilient and steadfast, as nature erodes.

A conductor of electricity, it's true,
Connecting the world, power flowing through,
In wires and cables, its purpose clear,
A lifeline of energy, without any fear.

In coins and currency, its value resides,
Unyielding and precious, it silently abides,

A testament to wealth, a symbol of worth,
Nickel's allure spreads across the earth.
    From stainless steel to batteries strong,
Nickel's versatility sings its own song,
In industrial machines and everyday gear,
Its presence is felt, crystal clear.
    A silent hero, hidden in plain sight,
Nickel shines with a radiant light,
A jewel of the periodic table's crown,
In chemistry's realm, it wears a majestic gown.
    So let us celebrate this metal divine,
A testament to resilience, a treasure to find,
Nickel, the element that never fades,
A symphony of strength, in every shade.

THIRTY-ONE

TECHNOLOGY AND INDUSTRY

In the realm of elements, Nickel stands tall,
A guardian of strength, it will never fall.
Resistance to rust, it defies decay,
Enduring the test of time, come what may.

A conductor of energy, vibrant and pure,
Its conductivity, a gift to endure.
Through wires and circuits, it flows with grace,
Powering the world, at an electrifying pace.

A symbol of progress, in technology and industry,
Nickel's presence, a testament to its supremacy.
In alloys and batteries, it finds its place,
Enhancing strength and efficiency with its embrace.

Malleable and elegant, it takes on any form,
Crafted into art, with beauty that'll transform.

From coins to jewelry, it adorns with grace,
A treasure to be cherished, in every case.
   Nickel, oh Nickel, a metal divine,
Your endurance and resilience forever shine.
A conductor, a guardian, a symbol of might,
You illuminate the world, with your radiant light.

THIRTY-TWO

STEADFAST AND PURE

In the realm of elements, Nickel does reside,
A metal that gleams with a radiant pride.
Conductivity courses through its veins,
A conductor supreme that never wanes.

Resistance to corrosion, a shield so strong,
Defying the rust that seeks to prolong.
In technology's grasp, it finds its place,
Empowering devices with its electrical embrace.

In the crucible of industry, it plays a role,
Forging alloys and compounds, a vital soul.
From stainless steel to batteries that power,
Nickel's versatility shines every hour.

In coins and currency, its value is seen,
A symbol of worth, a nation's gleam.

Hidden in pockets, purses, and wallets,
A silent presence, unnoticed by many.
    Yet in everyday life, its touch is near,
In kitchen appliances and machinery we steer.
From plating to magnets, it lends its grace,
An element of wonder in every space.
    Oh, Nickel, you endure with strength and might,
Powering the world, shining in the light.
Your beauty, elegance, forever allure,
A metal of wonder, steadfast and pure.

THIRTY-THREE

BEAUTY SO FINE

In the heart of technology, Nickel shines bright,
A conductor of currents, a guiding light.
With electrons flowing through its veins,
It powers the world, without any strains.

Resistant to corrosion, it stands so strong,
Braving the elements, where others go wrong.
Unyielding to rust, it stands the test of time,
With beauty and strength, forever sublime.

Oh, Nickel, you're a metal so pure,
Enduring and steadfast, that's for sure.
Malleable and flexible, you can take any form,
From coins to wires, you're the essence of norm.

Versatile and precious, you're valued so high,
In industries aplenty, where dreams touch the sky.

From aerospace to medicine, you play a key role,
A silent hero, silently taking its toll.

In the depths of the Earth, you're carefully found,
Mined with precision, from the underground.
Unearthed and refined, your brilliance revealed,
A treasure so rare, with secrets concealed.

Oh, Nickel, you're a gift from above,
A symbol of progress, a testament to love.
With conductivity and strength, you pave the way,
For a future that's bright, for a brand new day.

So let us celebrate Nickel, with all its might,
For it powers our world, both day and night.
A metal so noble, a beauty so fine,
Oh Nickel, forever may you shine.

THIRTY-FOUR

MYSTERIES UNFOLD

In the realm of elements, a treasure lies,
A metal of strength, where greatness lies,
Nickel, the conductor of electric might,
With versatility and endurance, shining bright.

An ally of copper, in alloys they dance,
Their union creating strength, a powerful stance,
Conductivity runs through its veins,
Harnessing energy, breaking the chains.

From wires that carry power's flow,
To coins that jingle and forever glow,
Nickel's value in currency we hold,
A symbol of wealth, a story untold.

In everyday life, it quietly resides,
A hidden presence, where strength hides,

From kitchen utensils to gleaming jewelry,
Nickel's touch bestows beauty and glee.
    In technology's realm, it finds its place,
An essential component, with grace,
From batteries that power our devices,
To intricate circuits, where knowledge entices.
    In industries vast, its role is profound,
From machinery to structures, it can be found,
Hidden in pockets and purses, unseen,
Nickel weaves its magic, a silent queen.
    In aerospace, it soars through the skies,
A shield against heat, where brilliance lies,
In medicine, it heals and mends,
A treasure from the Earth, where life transcends.
    Oh Nickel, you shine with strength and might,
A metal of wonders, a radiant light,
Enduring, versatile, and forever bold,
In your presence, the mysteries unfold.

THIRTY-FIVE

AEROSPACE AND MEDICINE

In the realm of technology, you shine bright,
With properties that bring forth endless delight.
Nickel, oh Nickel, a metal so pure,
Your presence in gadgets, we cannot ignore.

From batteries to magnets, you play your part,
Powering devices with a spark and a start.
In electronics, you're a conductor supreme,
Transmitting energy with an electric gleam.

In industry, you're a pillar of strength,
With alloys that endure, no matter the length.
Stainless steel, your creation, so strong and resilient,
Building structures that stand, a testament brilliant.

Oh Nickel, how you adorn our daily life,
In jewelry and coins, causing no strife.

With a lustrous shine, you capture our gaze,
A symbol of wealth, in so many ways.
  But beyond the surface, your worth runs deep,
In compounds and catalysts, secrets you keep.
As a catalyst, you speed up reactions in a blaze,
Helping industries thrive, in countless ways.
  In aerospace and medicine, you're a treasure,
Your strength and corrosion resistance, beyond measure.
From rocket engines to implants in bones,
You're a vital element, where progress is sown.
  Nickel, oh Nickel, you hold a special place,
In the tapestry of life, with grace and embrace.
A symbol of endurance, versatility, and might,
You are truly a gift, in the Earth's precious light.

THIRTY-SIX

HIDDEN GEM

In the heart of technology, a hidden gem,
A metal, strong and lustrous, we call it Nickel.
Forged in the depths of Earth's fiery realm,
Its presence felt in every industry's pickle.

    From skyscrapers to bridges, it lends its might,
Structures sturdy, steadfast, withstanding time.
A catalyst for progress, shining so bright,
Its touch in every invention, truly sublime.

    In batteries it resides, a potent force,
Powering our devices, day and night.
From smartphones to cars, it stays on course,
Driving us forward, with its glowing light.

    In coins and jewelry, its beauty shines,
An element of value, a metal divine.

Hidden in plain sight, it often reclines,
But its worth, undeniable, it does define.
    Oh Nickel, you're a catalyst of change,
A silent hero in every field you grace.
In aerospace and medicine, you rearrange,
Speeding up reactions, leaving no trace.
    So let us celebrate this element true,
With its versatility and strength untold.
Nickel, dear Nickel, we honor you,
For you're the backbone of our world, bold.

ABOUT THE AUTHOR

Walter the Educator is one of the pseudonyms for Walter Anderson. Formally educated in Chemistry, Business, and Education, he is an educator, an author, a diverse entrepreneur, and he is the son of a disabled war veteran. "Walter the Educator" shares his time between educating and creating. He holds interests and owns several creative projects that entertain, enlighten, enhance, and educate, hoping to inspire and motivate you.

Follow, find new works, and stay up to date
with Walter the Educator™
at WaltertheEducator.com

www.ingramcontent.com/pod-product-compliance
Lightning Source LLC
LaVergne TN
LVHW051958060526
838201LV00059B/3718